FACE TO FACE WITH
GRIZZLIES

by Joel Sartore

NATIONAL
GEOGRAPHIC

WASHINGTON, D.C.

← *I'm not often caught on camera, preferring to be behind it.*

FACE TO FACE

← *Opening wide, a bear that's trained for the movie industry pretends to roar up a tree in exchange for chunks of salmon.*

It was the Fourth of July, and there were brown bears all around me. In the woods behind, in the stream below, there were at least 20 of them, all with one thing on their mind—salmon. These were the famous fishing bears of Brooks Falls, Alaska.

Thousands of tourists and photographers come here each year. They try to get the perfect picture of a bear grabbing a waterfall-leaping salmon in mid-air. It's one of the few places where these

HOW TO NOT GET EATEN BY A GRIZZLY

- To avoid surprising a bear, sing songs, talk loudly, and call out "hey bear" when hiking in bear country.

- Hang food between trees at campsites.

- Never run from a bear.

- Give bears the space they need.

often solitary animals gather. They come to feed on the thousands of fish that pool up at the base of a waterfall. The bears have an understanding with the tourists. Nobody gets hurt.

This was my third day on assignment for NATIONAL GEOGRAPHIC magazine. It was the first day I thought I might not live through the job.

It was getting dark, so I began to head back to camp. It was a mile (1.6 kilometer) hike to my tent. I didn't even make it 40 feet (12 meters) when I saw her—a big female with two cubs. They were up on a hillside behind the viewing platform. They were feeding on a big sockeye salmon she'd carried up from the stream.

I was downhill, just stepping off the platform's boardwalk onto the trail. She didn't like that. In seconds she bounded down the hill, head down, mouth foaming. She was braced, ready to spring. She didn't roar; her mouth was closed. Her stare was intense.

They tell you not to run if a grizzly charges you. That was not a problem for me. I didn't remember that I even had legs at that point. I lowered my eyes, apologized softly, and slowly backed up. The standoff lasted only ten seconds or so. She snorted

and trotted back up the hill. She gathered her fish and her cubs, and went off into the woods. I sat down, shaking. I'd been charged by a grizzly.

Welcome to the world of the grizzly bear. I've spend two years with them in the field. Though I'm no expert, I can spread the word about what I've seen first-hand. This is a story of the Great Bear—and what's at stake if we lose it.

MEET

A pair of nearly grown siblings on the beach coast of Katmai National Park, Alaska.

THE GRIZZLY

A big male rests while guarding food in Alaska. Bears conceal their partially eaten prey with sticks or leaves until it's time to feed again.

The first thing you should know is that grizzly bears and brown bears are the same species—the group scientists call *Ursus arctos*. The bears that live along the coasts may have a dark brown coat and get a little bigger because they've got salmon to eat. People often call them brown bears. The bears that live inland are generally smaller and may have light-tipped, or grizzled, fur. People often call them grizzly bears. Brown bears live around the world, but grizzly bears are North American.

9

In this book, I use the names brown bears and grizzlies interchangeably to talk about North American bears.

The second thing you should know is that brown bears are omnivorous—they'll eat almost anything from salmon to garbage. They're not picky, just hungry.

The third thing you should know is that their diet does not include humans. Bear attacks are

Range of Brown Bear
in North America

⬆ *Grizzly bears used to roam as far south as Mexico. Today, they are mainly found in Alaska and Canada.*

➡ *A bear leaves the beach at low tide at Hallo Bay, a remote area of the Alaska coastline.*

A bear catches a nap. Napping is different from the deep sleeplike state of hibernation. When hibernating, bears don't need to eat, drink, or urinate.

A mother nurses her young. Cubs will stay with their mothers for about two years, learning how to forage for plants, fish, and other game. During this time they also learn how to avoid danger from other bears and, hopefully, humans.

rare. On average, only one to two people are killed each year by grizzlies. Your odds of getting struck by lightning are much higher. Some 70 people die from lightning strikes in the United States each year.

Knowing bears' annual life cycle may help you understand them better. In winter bears spend much of their time in dens in a sleeplike state, called hibernation. Nature invented hibernation as a way for bears to use less energy when food is scarce. When hibernating, they don't need to eat at all. How long they hibernate depends on where they live. In some places along the coast, some bears don't hibernate much at all because there is always something to eat. In the Arctic, some bears

↑ *Two bears nuzzle curiously, perhaps engaging in courtship behavior. Bears are playful and curious, and each one has an individual personality. That's just one reason why I find them so fascinating.*

hibernate seven months of the year. Needless to say, they eat non-stop during the other five months.

Mating and breeding can take place at any time in the late spring and early summer. The young are born in the den during hibernation. They stay with their mother an average of two years before she runs them off. Then the cycle begins again.

13

BEAR'S LIFE

Grizzlies spend much of their lives all by themselves. But they are social animals at times. Mothers and cubs, older siblings, and even unrelated bears often investigate things together. Grizzlies can be very playful and have a strong sense of curiosity. They tend to gather in groups around food sources. That's when things can get tense. Generally the biggest males feed first. Younger bears worry constantly about being attacked. They are often seen around the edges of feeding areas. Mother bears are extra careful around

→ *Early each spring, many bears will eat anything they can get. Some spend hours digging for small clams at low tide along coastlines.*

↑ *A bear's eyes shine gold as it swims after salmon in Alaska. Many bears feed at night, including this fishing bear with its salmon prize.*

other bears, because other bears sometimes kill cubs.

In the spring, look for bears feeding on tender new grasses in meadows or digging for small clams along beaches. In the summer, bears gather to feed on salmon in shallow streams and rivers. They also eat elk, bison and moose calves, and berries. In the fall they eat fish, roots and bulbs, pine seeds, and moths. The waking months—from late spring through summer, and fall—are when they need to put on fat for the winter. Some gain 200 pounds (91 kilograms) or more.

The later into the fall it gets, the more bears eat, almost around the clock at times. They are preparing for winter's hibernation. Most bears dig or find a cave, either high on a mountainside or in an Arctic snowbank. Then they fall into their sleeplike state. When it warms up outside, they go back to looking for food. This pattern of a bear's life will repeat itself for as long as the bear lives—and some wild bears live to be 30.

So how do we know all this? Because biologists have been studying bears for decades. *Ursus arctos*

A bear chases a bison calf in Yellowstone. This is a rare photograph of a bear chasing its prey.

is big, active during the day, and easy to watch with a good pair of binoculars.

Besides studying bears in person, biologists use special collars or ear tags that pinpoint bears' movements. Radio collars send out a radio signal nearly 30 miles (48 kilometers) away. GPS (Global Positioning System) collars and satellite collars communicate with satellites circling high above the Earth. This information is used to track bears anywhere. At any given time, biologists can see exactly where a bear is in its habitat, and whether it's on the move or not. The collars fall off, usually after a few years.

The information gleaned from tracking tells where the bears' favorite feeding areas are, how far they range, even where they hibernate through the winter. All of this knowledge is vital in knowing which habitats to protect in order to keep bear populations healthy.

Bear biologist Dick Shideler checks a tranquilized bear after putting a radio collar on the animal in Alaska.

HOW TO COLLAR A BEAR

- Catch the bear in a baited cage or track him from a helicopter.

- Dart the bear with a tranquilizer.

- Check the bear's health and take blood samples.

- Put on the collar or ear tag to track the bear's movement.

- Track the collared bear when he awakes—from a safe distance!

INTO

A mother bear watches her two cubs attempt to climb into a garbage dumpster.

THE FUTURE

A curious bear meets a vehicle at Yellowstone Bear World in Idaho. Here visitors can drive among bears—so long as they don't get out of their cars.

Grizzlies once ranged all over western North America and even down into northern Mexico. By the late 1800s, people had killed most of the bears in this range. The only survivors lived in pockets of mountainous habitat too rugged for humans to settle.

Today, even the mountains have become a tough place for a bear to make a living. Many of the mountain valleys of the American West now have roads and houses in them. People have settled in nearly every area imaginable,

➡ *Bears and tourists coexist peacefully at Brooks Falls, Alaska, home to the famous fishing bears. The more than 50,000 visitors a year are often referred to as the "bear paparazzi."*

DON'T FEED THE BEARS

In bear country, "a fed bear is a dead bear," so, if you live there or visit there:

— **Lock up your garbage.**

— **Put away bird feeders.**

— **Don't leave dog food out in the open.**

— **If you see a bear, don't panic! Just call the authorities.**

leaving very few places for bears to feed.

Grizzlies cannot find much food on the tops of snow- and ice-covered peaks. They must go down into the valleys to search for game and plants. This is becoming more and more of a problem. The remaining forests are disappearing as trees are cut for wood. The valleys are becoming built up with houses. Bears are extremely smart and resourceful. Many—though not all—can tolerate people surprisingly well much of the time. The problem is that many people do not understand bear behavior and can't tolerate bears close to them. This must change if grizzly bears are to survive in the long run.

Currently, grizzly bears in the U.S. lower 48 states are listed as a threatened species. They exist mainly in two areas: in and around Yellowstone and Glacier National Parks. There are

↑ *Specially bred to bark up a storm, Karelian bear dogs train on a dead grizzly in Montana. The dogs are used to scare bears out of towns and suburbs.*

other places where bears exist in the lower 48, but their numbers are few, and they often live far apart from other bear populations. The bears in Canada are not faring much better. The province of Alberta may soon decide to import bears, perhaps from the United States.

Isolation from other bears is the main problem that bears face in the long term. In the past, most places that bears lived were connected. Connected bear populations mingled and made each other stronger. Bears from the different populations would mate with each other to improve diversity. Now, with highways, cities, and development spreading out all across the West, bear populations are cut off from each other.

When fire or disease kill many of the bears in an isolated bear population, no nearby bears can come in to mate and increase numbers. This leaves the bear population weak. This weakening may become so serious that it will cause the wild populations to fail.

Things look much better for the grizzly bear in Alaska. A great deal of habitat has been set aside there, and it shows. Bear hunting is allowed, but biologists guess that the populations there remain strong at about 30,000 animals. Time will tell.

HOW
YOU CAN
HELP

⬆ *This wildlife overpass in Alberta, Canada, is an example of how humans can share space with bears and other animals.*

THE BEST WAY YOU CAN HELP SAVE grizzly bears is to be better informed. Read all that you can about them, and form your own opinions about this animal and its fate. The more information you have on the subject, the better.

▬ Let your parents know you care about bears, and ask them if they feel the same way. If so, then perhaps they will vote for politicians who have the same views. If elected officials know that saving wildlife is important to voters, they'll work harder to protect it.

▬ There are several groups that work to buy land to prevent development and save the last of the grizzly's habitat. One of these groups is Vital Ground in Montana. The Nature Conservancy is buying land to save ecosystems as well. Groups such as these offer the most immediate way of supporting the last of the wild bears.

▬ Grizzly bears are a keystone species. This means that they act as a foundation for the ecosystem in which they live. They use a variety of habitats at different times of the year. When we preserve forests, meadows, streams, and coastal areas for bears, it benefits all the other species that live there as well.

▬ Whether you are a fan of songbirds, eagles, wolves, or flowers, saving habitat is what it's all about. Protecting entire ecosystems is truly the best way to save all creatures from extinction. And since we human beings are totally dependent on the natural world for our own survival, when we save other species, we are saving ourselves.

▬ The future of this magnificent animal is in our hands now. Bears can exist only where we allow them to and nowhere else. Can this animal continue to thrive in the wild? Yes, but only if enough of us care to save it.

AN ARMCHAIR ADVENTURE*

⬇ *Bears and their cuddly appearance led to the creation of the famous teddy bear, named for President Theodore (Teddy) Roosevelt.*

JUST IMAGINE YOU ARE A PHOTOGRAPHER and are given an assignment to take pictures of grizzlies. Where should you go? How do you think you will take the best pictures? How can you apply what you've learned in this book to your assignment? Collect your data in a notebook to help plan your trip and your strategy. Make checklists of what to bring and what to look for in the field. Organize and plan carefully!

1 You know what bears eat and how they find their food. How will this help you find bears in the wild?

2 What should you do if you see a grizzly?

3 What qualities do you think will help you succeed as a bear photographer? What equipment would help?

4 Scientists have told you that photographing hibernating bears is extremely dangerous. Why do you think this is? What might the bears do when they wake up?

5 Do your homework and stay safe. You might bring home some pictures to publish!

* You know you can't <u>really</u> go on assignment in the field until you are at least 18 and have plenty of training!

FACTS
AT A
GLANCE

⬆ *A silvery cub shows off classically "grizzled" fur. This look led to the name, "grizzlies."*

Scientific Name
Ursus arctos

Common names
Don't be confused: Grizzly bears are also called brown bears depending on where they live—but these bears are not the same as American black bears (*Ursus americanus*).

Nicknames
grizzlies, silvertips

Coat
A brown bear's fur can be anywhere from dark brown to blond. Named for the white-tipped hairs of their fur, grizzlies can appear grizzled or gray.

Size
Height: 3 to 4 ½ feet (0.9 to 1.4 meters) at the shoulder.
Length: 5 ½ to 9 ½ feet (1.7 to 2.9 meters). *Weight:* Males are larger than females and can weigh as much as 1,400 pounds (635 kilograms). Males along the coast have more to eat and weigh about 800 pounds (363 kilograms). Males in the interior weigh less, around 320 pounds

(145 kilograms). Females weigh about two-thirds as much. After hibernation, bears may have lost a third of their body weight.

Claws
Can reach 4 inches (10 centimeters) in length on their front paws.

Diet
Bears are omnivorous, which means they eat almost anything. Brown bears eat grasses and berries, nuts and grubs, small animals and fish, and even large mammals. A brown bear can eat as much as 90 pounds (40 kilograms) of food a day!

Reproduction
Female bears are usually four to six years old when they have their first cubs. They give birth to one to three cubs while hibernating. At birth, the cubs weigh only a pound (0.5

28

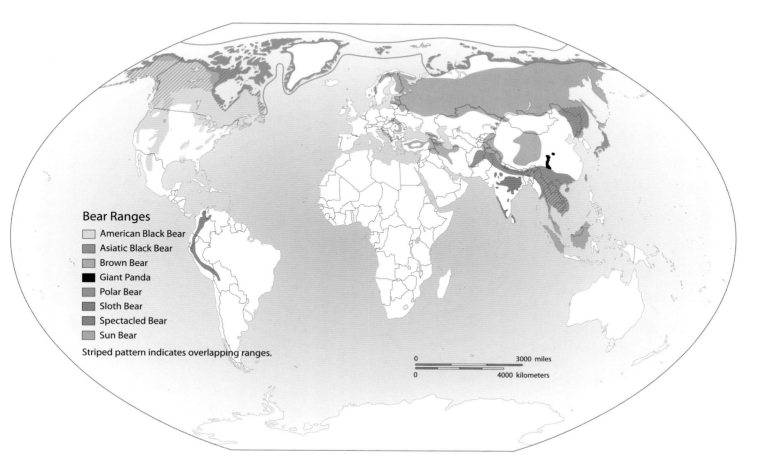

Bear Ranges

- American Black Bear
- Asiatic Black Bear
- Brown Bear
- Giant Panda
- Polar Bear
- Sloth Bear
- Spectacled Bear
- Sun Bear

Striped pattern indicates overlapping ranges.

| 0 | | 3000 miles |
| 0 | | 4000 kilometers |

kilograms). They grow from drinking their mother's milk. The cubs stay with their mother for two or three years. Then she sends them off on their own.

Status in the wild

Grizzly bears are not currently an endangered species, but they are listed as threatened in the lower 48 states.

Lifespan

Brown bears can reach 25 to 30 years of age in the wild.

Individual home range

For male grizzlies the area they may call home can be as big as one thousand square miles (2,590 square kilometers). Most home ranges are quite a bit smaller.

Eight species of bears roam the world.

Brown bear range

North America, Europe, and Asia. Grizzlies only live in North America. Brown bears live in forested mountains, river valleys, and meadows, in tundra and along the coast.

GLOSSARY

cub: a bear less than a year old

ecosystem: the animals, plants, and natural resources that make up a unit in nature

habitat: the area where an animal or plant is normally found

hibernation: an inactive, sleep-like state. Bears hibernate throughout the winter months to survive long periods without food or water.

home range: the area in which a bear lives

keystone species: a species that acts as the centerpiece in an ecosystem. Without the keystone species, the ecosystem suffers and could even collapse.

mammal: an animal whose young drink milk from their mother and usually has hair covering its body. Humans are mammals.

omnivorous: feeding on both vegetation and animals

species: a group of living things that look like one another and are able to reproduce.

FIND OUT MORE

Books & Articles

Betz, Dieter. *The Bear Family*. Tambourine Books, New York, 1992.

Chadwick, Douglas. "Grizzlies," NATIONAL GEOGRAPHIC magazine (July 2001), pp. 2-25.

Chadwick, Douglas. *True Grizz: Glimpses of Fernie, Stahr, Easy, Dakota, and Other Real Bears in the Modern World*. Sierra Club Books, New York, 2003.

Gibbons, Gail. *Grizzly Bears*. Holiday House, New York, 2003.

⬆ *Why did this bear in Yellowstone cross the road?*

Gilks, Helen. *Bears*. Ticknor & Fields, New York, 1993.

Hirschi, Ron. *Searching for Grizzlies*, Boyds Mill Press, Honesdale, Pa., 2005.

Murray, John. *Grizzly Bears: An Illustrated Field Guide*. Roberts Rinehart, Boulder, Colorado, 1995.

Web Sites

Canadian Wildlife Federation: http://www.cwf-fcf.org/

Defenders of Wildlife: http://www.defenders.org/

Get Bear Smart Society: http://www.bearsmart.com/

IUCN (International Union for the Conservation of Nature and Natural Resources): http://www.iucn.org/

National Wildlife Federation: http://www.nwf.org/

Nature Conservancy: http://www.nature.org/

North American Bear Center: http://www.bear.org/

Sierra Club: http://www.sierraclub.org/

Vital Ground: http://www.vitalground.org/

Wilderness Society: http://www.wilderness.org/

Wildlife Conservation Society: http://www.wcs.org/

Wind River Bear Institute http://www.beardogs.org/

World Wildlife Fund: http://www.worldwildlife.org/

INDEX

RESEARCH & PHOTOGRAPHIC NOTES

On all of the shoots in this book, I was seldom alone. I knew that working by myself in bear country was a foolish thing to do. The odds of being attacked by a bear decrease considerably if you're with a group of people. Surprising a bear when you're all alone is asking for trouble.

For example, I spent a good deal of time at Brooks Falls, where many people go to safely see the famous fishing bears each summer. When choosing a place less frequently visited by the public, I hired good guides and field assistants who knew what they were doing. We made noise when we walked so as to avoid surprise encounters. We kept a clean camp, cooking well away from our tents where we would sleep. Above all, we did our homework. Bear attacks are extremely rare. I wanted to keep it that way.

As for what kind of gear to take in bear country, I always packed plenty of sunscreen, bug repellent, rain gear, water, and food. It's hard to do good work when you're miserable, and nothing is worse than being soaking wet or hungry for days on end.

The photographic gear was a bit more complicated, but equally important, of course. I always travel with several cameras and a wide variety of lenses, from a nearly-fish eye wide angle to a 600mm lens. You never know what you're going to need on any given day. Also, I seldom carry a camera bag because they are too hard on your shoulders after awhile. A shooting vest with many pockets more evenly distributes the weight of all that gear, and frees up your hands for focusing and firing the camera.

The most important ingredient to any shoot, however, is simply to have fun. The more you enjoy yourself as you're shooting, the better your pictures will be. If you do your research and study bear behavior before leaving home, you'll know how to maintain a safe and respectful distance from your furry subjects. That's good for everyone, bears and humans alike. —JS

FOR MY WIFE, KATHY,
AND OUR THREE CUBS. —JS

Acknowledgments:
This book would not have been possible without the help of many biologists, guides, and conservationists including Doug Chadwick, Kerri Hunt, Tim Manley, Doug and Lynne Seus, Derek Reich, and Dick Shideler. These people fight the same fights, year in, year out, to save what's left of the natural world. I am humbled by their caring, dedication, and knowledge.—JS

The publisher gratefully acknowledges the assistance of Christine Kiel, K-3 curriculum and reading consultant; Hillary Robison at the University of Nevada; Dr. Stephen Herrero, professor emeritus of environmental science at the University of Calgary; and Dr. Michael Vaughan, professor of wildlife at Virginia Tech.

Page 5 photograph copyright © Jim Webb. Back cover photograph copyright © Otto Ty Kendall and Scott Handley.

Book design by David M. Seager
The body text of the book is set in ITC Century. The display text is set in Knockout and Party Noid.

Published by the
National Geographic Society

John M. Fahey, Jr., *President and Chief Executive Officer*

Gilbert M. Grosvenor, *Chairman of the Board*

Nina D. Hoffman, *Executive Vice President, President of Books*

Staff for This Book

Nancy Laties Feresten, *Vice President, Editor-in-Chief of Children's Books*

Bea Jackson, *Design and Illustrations Director, Children's Books*

Jennifer Emmett, *Project Editor*

David M. Seager, *Art Director*

Lori Epstein, *Illustrations Editor*

Michelle Harris, *Researcher*

Jean Cantu, *Illustrations Specialist*

Carl Mehler, *Director of Maps*

Rebecca Baines, *Editorial Assistant*

Kate Olesin, *Intern*

R. Gary Colbert, *Production Director*

Lewis R. Bassford, *Production Manager*

Vincent P. Ryan, *Manufacturing Manager*

Cover: A Kodiak bear stares me down near Larsen Bay, Alaska. *Back Cover:* I am kissed by trained bears in California. *Page One:* A famous Brooks Falls, Alaska, fishing bear. *Title Page:* Face to face with a grizzly. *Credits page:* A playful bear rolls in fall colors in Alaska.

Library of Congress
Cataloging-in-Publication Data

Sartore, Joel.
  Face to face with grizzlies / by Joel Sartore.
     p. cm. -- (Face to face)
  Includes bibliographical references.
  ISBN-13: 978-1-4263-0050-9 (hardcover)
  ISBN-13: 978-1-4263-0051-6 (library binding)
  1. Grizzly bear--North America. I. Title.
  QL737.C27S257 2006
  599.784--dc22

2006020500

One of the world's largest nonprofit scientific and educational organizations, the National Geographic Society was founded in 1888 "for the increase and diffusion of geographic knowledge." Fulfilling this mission, the Society educates and inspires millions every day through its magazines, books, television programs, videos, maps and atlases, research grants, the National Geographic Bee, teacher workshops, and innovative classroom materials. The Society is supported through membership dues, charitable gifts, and income from the sale of its educational products. This support is vital to National Geographic's mission to increase global understanding and promote conservation of our planet through exploration, research, and education.

For more information, please call
1-800-NGS-LINE (647-5463)
or write to the following address:

National Geographic Society
1145 17th Street N.W.
Washington, D.C. 20036-4688
U.S.A.

Visit the Society's Web site:
www.nationalgeographic.com

Printed in China